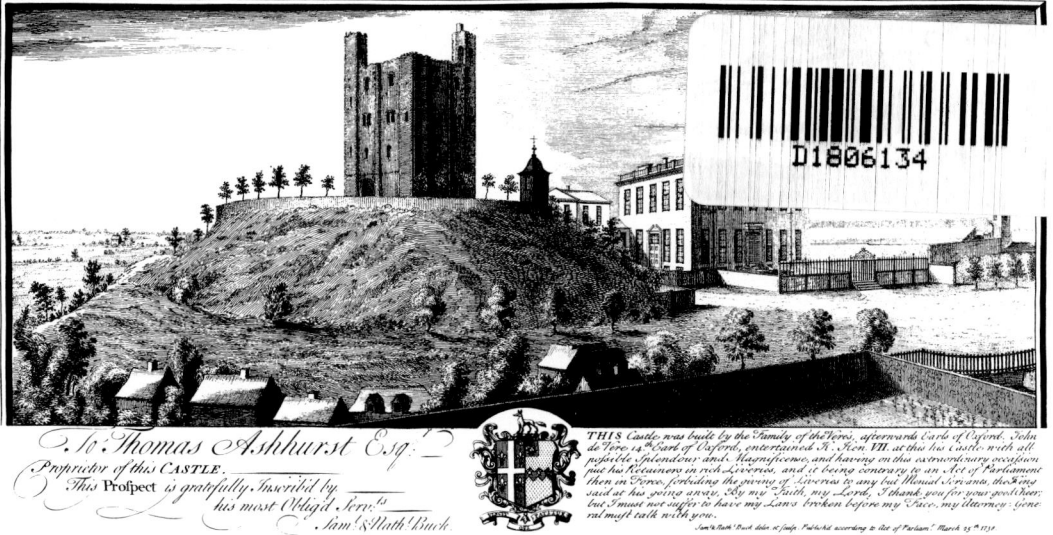

To Thomas Ashhurst Esq.
Proprietor of this CASTLE.
This Prospect *is gratefully Inscribed by*
his most Oblig'd Serv.ts
Sam.l & Nath.l Buck.

THIS Castle was built by the Family of the Veres, afterwards Earls of Oxford. John de Vere 14.th Earl of Oxford, entertained K. Hen. VII. at this his Castle with all possible Splendour and Magnificence, and having on this extraordinary occasion put his Retainers in rich Liveries, and it being contrary to an Act of Parliament then in Force, forbiding the giving of Liveries to any but Menial Servants, the King said at his going away, By my Faith, my Lord, I thank you for your good cheer; but I must not suffer to have my Laws broken before my Face, my Attorney-General must talk with you.

Sam.l & Nath.l Buck delin. et sculp. Published according to Act of Parliam.t March 25.th 1735.

The Buck brothers' view of Hedingham in 1730. Opposite: 19th century watercolour of the Keep

HEDINGHAM CASTLE

Hedingham Castle's great Norman keep is among the most magnificent and best preserved in Europe. It was built by Aubrey de Vere in about 1140 and stands as an enduring monument to this illustrious but now extinct family.

The walls of the keep are immensely strong, being twelve feet thick at the base and ten feet at the top. The East wall is one foot thicker than the other three, probably as protection against the prevailing East wind, or against the possibility of attack coming from the bridge side. The facing Ashlar stone had to be transported all the way from the quarries of Barnack in Northampton-shire. Because of the great difficulties of transportation it is not surprising that hardly any of the Norman Castles were completely faced with stone, like Hedingham. There were few nobles as rich and powerful as the de Veres who were able to afford the cost, and normally only the doors and windows were faced with cut stone.

Within the inner and outer facing is an infill of local flints and rubble bound together with a fluid mortar; a mixture of sand, lime and water.

The small holes on the exterior were mainly for the fixing of wooden scaffolding poles during the original construction of the building. Some of the regularly spaced gaps near the battlements are 'put-log holes' which were to take beams thrust through the wall to support wooden planks and hoardings. This gave the archers greater mobility and a wider field of fire in times of siege. Planks could also be lifted and molten pitch or boiling oil poured down upon the heads of the enemy.

The Castle is approached from the East by a beautiful Tudor bridge built by the 13th Earl of Oxford in 1496. This spans the dry moat and would have replaced the original drawbridge. Norman castles were usually built with an inner and outer bailey, the keep and the most important buildings being on the inner bailey, and those of lesser importance being on the outer bailey. Both of these would originally have had a curtain wall built round them; the Tudor bridge joins them together.

The surroundings of the Castle were kept clear of all scrub and trees so that no cover would

1

The largest Norman arch in Europe

be given to an approaching enemy. The trees which exist today were planted in about 1719 when Hedingham gave up all pretence of being a military fortification and became a gentleman's residence. It was at this date that the two large entrances were knocked into the East side of the keep. From the bridge a path crosses the inner bailey to the west side of the keep and a stone staircase leads up to the splendid arched doorway. At one time these stone steps were covered by a small tower attached to the main building. This gave considerable protection to the main entrance from battering-rams and other siege weapons, and would have made a direct attack impossible. The facing stone has been removed, and the remains of the tower are of flint and rubble. The keep has channels cut into it where the tower was keyed in, which probably shows that this was a later addition.

The roofless chamber outside the main door was the dungeon, and it is thought that the unlucky prisoners were lowered into this dark and gloomy hole through a trapdoor in the ceiling.

The main doorway has a well-defined chevron moulding above it and this typical Norman pattern is repeated on the exterior above the top windows, and also in the Banqueting Hall where there are particularly fine examples. Over the door there is a groove down which the portcullis would have slid, this was raised and lowered by a system of winches from the floor above. Inside the doorway there are holes cut in the wall on both sides into which draw bars were slid for reinforcement.

The entrance to the keep is on the first floor instead of the ground floor, as yet another precaution against attack. This is the Garrison, or Guard Room. The soldiers lived here, the armourer would have had his forge and the cooking was also done on this level. A great deal of noise and activity can be imagined. The windows are extremely narrow, sufficient to let in some light and to allow the archers to fire their arrows out, but not wide enough for missiles to penetrate. In the north east corner is the garderobe (lavatory), and in the north west corner is the beautiful spiral staircase leading downwards to the ground floor and upwards to the Banqueting Hall. The ground floor was used for storing food and provisions and as this was the level most vulnerable to attack there are no windows, only slits for air. It is cool and dark and the immense thickness of the walls keep the temperature almost constant.

There is thought to have been a well inside the keep, also a tunnel which emerged near the fishponds. A story goes that once, when Hedingham was under siege, soldiers in the keep threw down fresh fish to show how well supplied they were.

Above : View down the spiral stair

Left : typical Norman archway

The spiral staircase is thirteen feet wide in circumference and beautifully constructed round a central column. The steps were originally of stone, but were replaced with bricks in the 16th century. The staircase was built in a clockwise direction to allow the defending soldiers to have their right hands free to wield their swords as they descended.

The next floor is known as the Banqueting Hall or Armoury. This is the most splendid room in the keep and the timbered ceiling is supported by a magnificent central arch twenty-eight feet wide. It rises to a height of twenty feet, springing from a handsome pillar on either side. The smaller arches and windows are richly

Hedingham in Victorian times

decorated with chevron moulding. The fireplace on the south wall is of simple but good design with a cone-shaped flue which contains two ducts near the top. These run straight through the wall and emerge on either side of a flat buttress. If the fire smoked, one or other opening could be blocked, depending on the direction of the wind. In the North East corner there is a continuation of the garderobe shaft. The winding mechanism for the portcullis was in the alcove to the right of the stairs near the entrance to the room. This Great Hall would have been used for entertaining, giving audiences and holding court, so it is natural that this is the part of the keep where the skill of the Norman masons was used to the greatest effect. There are many different patterns to be found decorating the windows and alcoves, and each mason used his own distinguishing mark, sometimes a star, a cross, or a triangle.

Twelve feet above floor level a gallery runs around the entire room, tunnelled within the thickness of the wall. This is where the minstrels and troubadors would have played, and from here spectators had an excellent view of what was going on below. A banquet observed from this gallery must have been a splendid sight. It is easy to imagine the de Vere of the day and his wife seated at the top table in front of the fire, with the other tables placed lengthwise down the Hall. The furniture would have been very simple consisting of trestle tables, benches and chests, and the floor covered in rushes locally cut from Rushley Green. The walls would be richly decorated with fine hangings and the whole scene bathed in warm flickering light from tallow candles. There was a park full of red deer so venison would be an important part of the menu, also pheasant and partridge. There must have been an immense amount of noise against which the musicians had to compete. In addition, travelling acrobats, conjurors and the Hedingham jesters would all be doing their best to keep the assembled company entertained.

The next storey is the Dormitory Floor; this large room was probably divided into partitions by rugs and hangings for sleeping and relaxing. Most people would have slept on straw on the floor, but the lord and his family probably had simple wooden beds. The ladies could retire here for peace and quiet, a good gossip and making embroidery. The soldiers and servants would have slept on the other floors below, either in the alcoves, or rolled up in their cloaks on the rushes, wherever a space could be found.

In 1592 a Survey of the property was made for Lord Burghley, and from this it is known that on the inner bailey, in addition to the Norman keep, a great many important Tudor buildings were built by the 13th Earl of Oxford. There was an

The fine Norman doorway forming the main entrance to the keep

enormous red brick tower to the West of the keep, a chapel, hall, bakehouse, kitchen and pantries. These have now all gone, but many of the materials have been used again, some in the church tower built by the 18th Earl of Oxford in 1621, and some in the mansion house built by Sir Robert Ashhurst in 1719. This house stands on the outer bailey, once the site of storehouses, barns, stables, granaries, the brewhouse and the wood yard. The Tilting Lawn was here, where the knights practised their military skills, and the Archery Butts were on a lower level near the fishponds. In 1868 Lewis Majendie, owner of the Castle, excavated the inner bailey working from the Survey, and he found many interesting foundations of both stone and brick.

SOME ACCOUNT OF THE DE VERES

'The de Veres, Earls of Oxford, were the longest and most illustrious line of nobles that England has seen' wrote Macaulay. They owned vast estates in ten counties and were among the flower of English chivalry during the Hundred Years' War. The hereditary office of Lord Great Chamberlain is still vested in their descendants and one of their number is considered by many to be the real author of the 'Shakespeare' plays. With the 20th and last Earl of Oxford, the male line of this noble house expired, 'entombed in the urns and sepulchres of mortality'.

The Lordship of Hedingham in pre-Conquest days belonged to a great Saxon thane named

Right: arms of the de Vere family: quarterly gules and or, in the first quarter a mullet argent

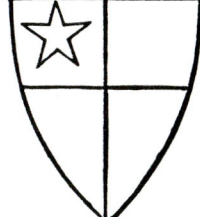

The Tudor bridge

5

Ulwine. He was one of those unfortunate people who did not benefit from the Norman invasion. William the Conqueror took all his lands and gave them to one of his best soldiers and most important knights, **Alberic (or Aubrey) de Ver.** He is thought to have been the Lord of Ver, which is below Coutances in the La Manche region of Normandy. In addition, de Vere was given fourteen Lordships in Essex, and land in Suffolk, Middlesex, Huntingdon and Cambridge. Even today London still bears traces of this famous family, such as de Vere Gardens in Kensington, (then Cheniston, where he was Lord of the Manor) and Earl's Court, where the de Veres had their court-house. Aubrey laid out four vineyards, one at Castle Hedingham, where wild red grapes have been found within the last century. He founded Earl's Colne Priory in 1105, and after the death of his wife became a monk, and died peacefully. Many of the Earls of Oxford were buried within the Priory walls. Aubrey married Beatrice, half-sister of King William, and they had five sons. It was their eldest son, Aubrey II, a great Crusader, who built the vast Norman Castle of Hedingham in about 1140, rather surprisingly using the Archbishop of Canterbury, William de Corbeuil, as architect.

There is a fine legend as to why the de Veres adopted the five-pointed star as their emblem. Aubrey was taking part in the first Crusade in 1098, and he and his troops were engaged in a fierce battle at Antioch with Admiral Corborant, Commander of the Sultan of Persia's forces. Dusk was falling and confusion was beginning to spread, but at the moment when the Saracens were about to be saved by the darkness, a brilliant five-pointed star appeared on the standard being carried by de Vere. The battlefield was illuminated, and a great victory won. The Star, or Mullet, as it is known, can be seen on many local churches and buildings connected with the de Vere family. Their arms: *quarterly gules and or, in the 1st quarter a mullet argent* are amongst the simplest and best known in medieval heraldry.

Aubrey II married Alice FitzRichard of Clare, daughter of the Earl of Hertford. He was referred to as 'the King's Chamberlain' in 1112,

and was created Lord Great Chamberlain of England in 1133. As such he attended King Stephen at Westminster and at Winchester in 1136. All subsequent holders of this great office of state were his descendants. His daughter Rohesia married Geoffrey de Mandeville, 1st Earl of Essex, and it is thought that this connection (Essex was extremely unpopular in London) may have contributed to Aubrey's death in a riot in London in 1141.

Aubrey de Vere III, another Crusader, was made an Earl by Queen Matilda, and he was offered the choice of title of Cambridge, "Provided the King of Scots had it not", Oxford, Berkshire, Wiltshire or Dorset. He chose Oxford, a title which continued for twenty generations. He was known as 'Aubrey the Grim' because of his height and stern appearance. As well as his title, he was given 'A third penny of the pleas of the county, as an Earl ought to have.' This **1st Earl of Oxford** married three times, and his third wife, Lucy, was greatly loved and founded a small Benedictine Nunnery in the village. No buildings remain, but there is still a Nunnery Street and a farm of the same name. Aubrey was a great friend and supporter of Queen Matilda who came to end her days at Hedingham, and died there on 3rd May, 1151.

Aubrey, 2nd Earl of Oxford, succeeded in 1194. He fought with Richard Coeur de Lion in Normandy, and later commanded King John's forces in Ireland. He was a Privy Councillor, and Steward of the Forest of Essex in 1213. When he died childless his brother Robert inherited.

Robert, 3rd Earl of Oxford was also a Crusader in the Holy Wars. In the fifteenth year of King John's reign, Robert took up arms against the King with twenty-five other barons 'in defence of the liberties of England', forcing him in 1215 to sign the Magna Carta. De Vere, like many others, was excommunicated for this action. The barons offered the crown to Louis, son of the King of France. A French force landed and established themselves in Colchester Castle, but King John attacked and the French surrendered. He then laid seige to Hedingham, which fell to him in Lent, 1216, after a long and fierce resistance. The following the

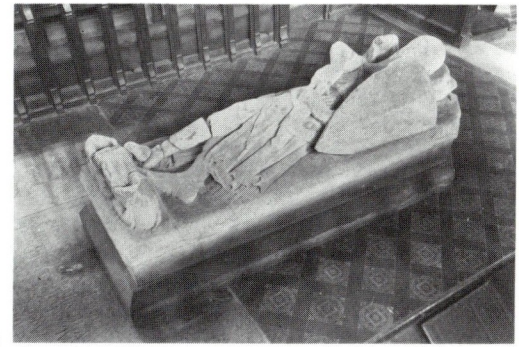

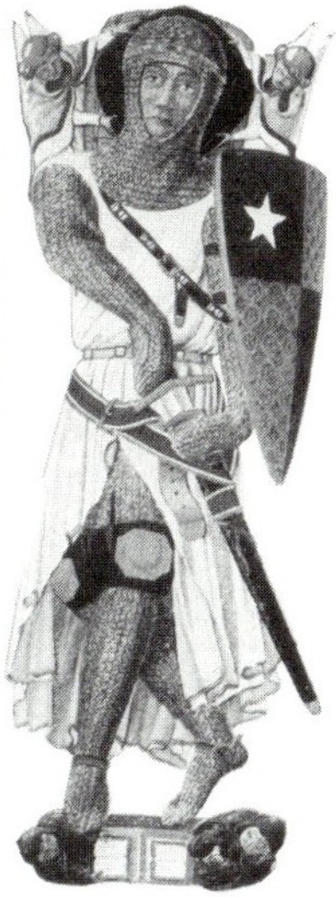

Left : King John who laid siege to Hedingham in 1216. Above : mutilated effigy of the 3rd Earl in Hatfield Braod Oak Church

Right : reconstruction of the 3rd Earl's effigy

Dauphin and his soldiers once more beseiged Hedingham, and after a desperate struggle it was finally re-taken. On the death of King John peace was made between King Henry III and the barons, Oxford was back in favour and Hedingham and all his lands were restored to him. He was buried at Hatfield Priory in 1221.

Distant view of Keep in the 18th century

Hugh, 4th Earl of Oxford, born in 1210, was at the side of King Edward I at the Siege of Caerlaverock. Later, he fought in the sixth Crusade from 1248 to 1254. He married Hawise de Quincy, daughter of the 1st Earl of Winchester, another of the Magna Carta barons. In about 1250 he founded a hospice or almshouse in Chapel Pasture near the Castle gates, "For the feeding and lodging of poor and impotent persons, and for the celebration of divine service for himself, his wife and his descendants." He also built the steeple of Earl's Colne church, and was buried there in 1263.

Robert de Vere, 5th Earl of Oxford, was Master Chamberlain of England and fought for Edward I against the Welsh. Through his wife, Alice de Saundford, the Earl claimed successfully to be Chamberlain in fee to Queen Eleanor. He died in 1296 and his beautiful effigy is now in the Chapel at Bures.

Effigy of Robert, 5th Earl of Oxford in St. Stephen's Chapel, Bures

Robert, 6th Earl of Oxford, was noted for his military prowess, and fought for Kings Edward I, II and III in France and Scotland. He officiated at the coronation of Queen Isabella, wife of Edward II, in 1308. Afterwards, as Great Chamberlain he was allowed to claim certain perquisites: the Queen's shoes and sandals, and three silver basins used for washing, but he accepted 100 marks in lieu of the bed upon which the Queen had spent the night before the coronation. He was known as "The Good Earl of Oxford, his Government, both in peace and war being so prudent, his Hospitality and Works of Charity so wisely abundant, and his Temperance, with a religious Zeal, so admirably conjoined, that the common People esteemed him as a Saint." His only son, Thomas, predeceased him, and he left his estates to his nephew John.

The martial tradition of the 'fighting Veres' was continued by **John, 7th Earl of Oxford.** A famous soldier, renowned for his gallantry, he was one of King Edward III's greatest generals. When war broke out with France Oxford put to sea with three great ships in November 1339 in the King's service.

At the Battle of Crecy he was one of the commanders of the first division with the Black Prince and the Earl of Warwick. During the Siege of Calais he was sent back to England to get horses and supplies, but was hastily recalled. He left England with two hundred ships, but fell into a great battle with a French fleet also bound for Calais. The French were defeated and he captured twenty ships and many galleys loaded with supplies. In 1356 he was again in command of the first division with Warwick at Poitiers, where Oxford's use of his archers contributed to the famous victory where King John (of France) was taken prisoner. "Yet all Courage had been thrown away to no Purpose, had it not been seconded by the extraordinary Gallantry of the English Archers, under the Earl of Oxford, who behaved themselves that Day with wonderful Constancy, Alacrity and Resolution."

When he was killed at the Siege of Rheims in January, 1360, the Earl left vast estates in ten counties.

Thomas, 8th Earl of Oxford, succeeded in 1360. He served with King Edward III and distinguished himself on the field of battle. His wife, Maud, was daughter and heir of Sir Ralph de Ufford, Chief Justice of Ireland. When he died in 1371 his Countess survived him by many years, and in 1404 she took part in a conspiracy in Essex against King Henry IV, spreading rumours that King Richard II was alive. She was arrested and sent to the Tower of London, but later pardoned.

In 1377, when ten year old King Richard II

went to his coronation in Westminster Abbey, fifteen year old **Robert de Vere, 9th Earl of Oxford** and Hereditary Chamberlain of England, was allowed to act as King's Chamberlain although still a minor. Robert, born in 1362, succeeded to his title when only nine. When aged 16 he married Philippa, daughter of the Earl of Bedford and granddaughter of Edward III, he became the King's cousin. De Vere was a brave man, as in June, 1381, when the government was in panic, he carried the King's sword and was at his side when young Richard rode out from the Tower of London to meet Wat Tyler and his peasants' army at Mile End. He had great influence with the King who showered honours upon him, and gave him additional estates. He created him Marquess of Ireland in 1385, and in the following year **Duke of Ireland,** with semi-regal powers. The royal dukes and other nobles became increasingly jealous of the rise of de Vere, and he caused great offence when he abandoned Philippa, his wife, and had one of the Queen's maidens abducted to live with him. This particularly incensed the Duke of Gloucester, Philippa's uncle. The nobles plotted against him and he was eventually forced into exile after being impeached for High Treason, and had all his lands confiscated. He escaped to Flanders in a fishing boat and took up residence at Utrecht. Later, King Richard contemplated bringing him back, but it was impossible. His mother visited him in 1391 and gave him some financial help, but the following year out hunting he was fatally injured by a boar. A sad end for one born to such greatness and good fortune. The King, grieving for his exiled friend, had the body brought back to England in a 'Cypress Case' for his funeral at Earl's Colne. The Archbishop of Canterbury took the solemn and magnificent ceremony, and the King had the coffin opened 'that he might look his last on his Favourite.' De Vere was apparelled in princely ornaments and robes, a gold chain placed round his neck and rings on his fingers, these were the King's wishes.

Aubrey, 10th Earl of Oxford, was uncle to the 9th who had died childless. He had nearly all the confiscated possessions restored to him, but

Upper part of effigy of the 10th Earl in Bures Chapel

Below : the 11th Earl and Countess in the Chapel at Bures

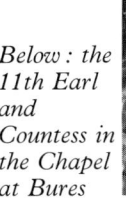

not the office of Great Chamberlain. Another 'fighting Vere', in 1367 he was retained to 'abide for life' with the Black Prince and received an allowance of 100 marks a year. He died in 1400 aged sixty, and his son Richard succeeded him.

Richard, 11th Earl of Oxford sailed to France with Henry V, his personal band being 39 men-at-arms and 60 archers. In 1415 he was one of the commanders at the Battle of Agincourt and a Knight of the Garter. Richard died in 1417 and was buried at Earl's Colne.

John, 12th Earl of Oxford, succeeded in 1417, like the 9th Earl, when only nine years old. He became a prominent Lancastrian and loyal to King Henry VI. On the accession of Edward IV, he and his eldest son came under suspicion and were arrested at Hedingham and imprisoned in the Tower of London. In 1461 both were beheaded on Tower Hill, Aubrey going to the

9

block in full view of his father. They were buried in Austin Friars church. The Earl was described as "A venerable old nobleman of unblemished character."

John, 13th Earl of Oxford, the 12th Earl's second son, was probably the greatest and richest of all the de Veres. He was 19 when his father and brother were executed. It is recorded that he was courageous, wise, learned and religious, also a great patron of the arts. Like his father he supported the Lancastrian cause and received most of his honours as reward for his bravery and leadership in the Wars of the Roses. In 1470 he and the Earl of Warwick marched to London to rescue the imprisoned King Henry VI from the Tower. King Edward fled, but the following year returned and landed in the North. When Oxford was fighting in the Battle of Barnet Field, just as victory seemed to be within reach, a terrible mistake was made by the Earl of Warwick's men, his allies. The mist came down and the de Vere star worn on his men's right shoulders was mistaken for the emblem of the sun worn by King Edward IV's men. They attacked, and with cries of 'Treason!' the Earl and his 800 men had to flee from the battlefield. The Yorkists recaptured King Henry and Edward IV returned to the throne. De Vere escaped to Scotland where on 28th April, 1471, the King of Scotland issued a safe-conduct for Oxford with forty Englishmen for six months. From Scotland he went to France where he assembled a squadron of ships and then caused havoc to the Yorkists' shipping. He returned to England in September, 1473, with 400 men, and captured St. Michael's Mount in Cornwall. The following year, after a long siege, he was forced to surrender to the King. He was taken prisoner and sent to Hammes Castle, near Calais, for twelve years. His wife, Margaret, was sister of the Earl of Warwick, another great enemy of the King, and as such she was treated with great cruelty. Deprived of all her income, she was never allowed to visit her husband, and was reduced to living on charity and on what she could earn from needlework. Saddest of all, their only child, John, died a prisoner in the Tower during his father's exile.

During this time, Hedingham Castle was

Henry VII who was entertained at Hedingham and later fined his host for putting too many of his servants into livery

granted to Sir Thomas Montgomery, but he was not able to enjoy it for very long. In 1485 de Vere escaped from Hammes; it is probable that the Governor was heavily bribed. He joined the Earl of Richmond and led the vanguard at the Battle of Bosworth Field in Leicestershire. The Yorkists were put to flight and Richmond was crowned King Henry VII. The Earl had all his possessions and property restored to him, and the new King gave him many titles and honours. He was the first person to be made a Knight of the Garter in the new reign. The hereditary office of Lord Great Chamberlain was renewed, and he was also made Constable of the Tower of London where he was Keeper of the King's Lions and Leopards, with a grant of 6d a day per beast. In addition he was Constable of Castle Rising and Lord High Admiral of England, Ireland and Aquitaine. The Castle had suffered during his long imprisonment but on his return he restored it to great splendour, adding many fine Tudor buildings and the lovely bridge which still survives. In 1491 he became godfather to the King's eldest son, the future King Henry VIII.

It was a few years later that King Henry VII was royally entertained at Hedingham and repaid his host with an act of great injustice. This famous story goes that at the King's departure all the servants stood in their livery, with coats emblazoned with the de Vere arms, and formed a lane down which the King passed. The King called the Earl and said to him, "My Lord, I have heard much of your hospitality, but

I see that it is greater than the speech. These handsome gentlemen and yeomen which I see on both sides of me are sure your menial servants?" The Earl smiled and answered, "If it may please your Grace, that were not for mine ease; they are most of them my retainers, that are come to do me service at such a time as this, and chiefly to see your Grace." The King startled a little and said, "By my faith, my Lord, I thank you for your good cheer, but I may not have my laws broken in my sight. My attorney must speak with you."

There was a law which stated that the nobles were only allowed a certain number of retainers to wear uniform or livery. This was an attempt to prevent any nobleman becoming too powerful and having his own private army. The Earl of Oxford had obviously exceeded the limit as he was fined the sum of 15,000 marks, the equivalent of a very large sum nowadays. As no-one had helped more than de Vere in raising the Earl of Richmond to the throne, the King might have overlooked the flouting of the law on this occasion, particularly as this heavy fine undoubtedly caused financial problems for the Earl and for his estate.

He died in 1512 and was buried in Colne Priory in the same tomb as his first wife.

"Little John of Camps", his nephew, became **14th Earl of Oxford** at the age of twelve and was made a ward of King Henry VIII. He lived at another de Vere estate, Castle Camps in Cambridgeshire. When he took charge of his inheritance in 1520, he became so extravagant that the King directed Wolsey to take over, and the Cardinal told de Vere to disperse his household and live with the Duke of Norfolk. He married the Duke's daughter, Anne Howard, but unfortunately it was a stormy marriage and the Cardinal ordered him to behave better towards his wife. He died, childless, just before his 27th birthday.

John, 15th Earl of Oxford was grandson of Sir George de Vere, and 2nd cousin of "Little John". He fought under Henry VIII, and was knighted by the King after the famous Battle of the Spurs in 1513. In 1520 he was with the King at the Field of the Cloth of Gold, and went with him to Dover two years later to meet the

The tomb of the 15th Earl of Oxford and his Countess, in black marble, which can be seen in the church at Castle Hedingham

Emperor Charles V. De Vere was bearer of the Crown at Anne Boleyn's coronation, and was at her trial in 1536. He also attended the funeral of Jane Seymour in 1537. In 1540 he and his son Lord Bulbeck were with Henry at Blackheath to

Two Oxford siblings – Lord Vere of Tilbury (left) a distinguished soldier, and Sir Francis Vere, Governor of Brill, grandsons of the 15th Earl

11

receive Anne of Cleves. He married Christian Fotheringay of Brockley, and was described by the Venetian Ambassador as 'a man of valour and authority, with a revenue of 25,000 ducats, whose custom it is always to cavalcade with 200 horse.' When he died in 1540 he was buried in Castle Hedingham church, where his imposing black marble tomb may be seen in the chancel. He was succeeded by his eldest son.

John, 16th Earl of Oxford, was born about 1516. Another fine soldier and, like his father, one of Henry VIII's generals, he greatly distinguished himself at the siege of Boulogne in 1544. He was one of the peers who signed on 16th June, 1553, settling the Crown on Lady Jane Grey, and before 19th July declared for Queen Mary. As Great Chamberlain he accompanied Mary on her progress through London on 30th September, and officiated at her coronation in November. In 1555 he was ordered by the Council to attend the burning of any heretics in Essex.

The Earl escorted Elizabeth from Hatfield to London when she became Queen, officiating at her coronation in 1559. His wife, Margery, was appointed a Maid of Honour to the new Queen, who came on a visit to Hedingham in 1561 when she was twenty-eight. She arrived on August 14th and departed on the 19th, going on to Gosfield Hall, then the home of Lord Rich. It must have been a great relief when a royal visit came to an end. The cost of a visit was very large as the Queen travelled with a huge retinue.

Lord Bulbeck (to become 17th Earl) was only eleven at the time, and must have been thrilled at meeting the Queen in his ancestral home. De Vere was a keen sportsman, and when Prince Eric of Sweden landed at Harwich he entertained him at Hedingham on his way to London. "After dinner my Lord Oxford had the Prince forth a-hawking and showed him great sport, killing in his sight both faisant and partridge." Small flat silver rings marked 'Oxforde' are occasionally found in the neighbourhood, these were fixed round the legs of the falcons.

When in France in 1544, de Vere astonished the French nobility at a boar hunt by killing the animal with a "dancing rapier". Such a hunt could be extremely dangerous and the Frenchmen were well armed and carried lances. Oxford, tired of hunting a large and fierce boar, dismounted and walked down a woodland path. Suddenly, the infuriated animal emerged in front of him and charged. The Frenchmen shouted to him to run and save himself, but de Vere drew his light rapier and slew the boar at the first encounter. The amazement of the French nobles greatly surprised the Earl who said, "My Lords, what have I done of which I have no feeling? Is it the killing of this English pig? Why, every boy in my nation would have performed it. They may be bugbears to the French; to us they are but servants."

At King Henry VIII's funeral Lord Oxford was one of the chief mourners. For a time he was much persecuted by the Duke of Somerset and was forced to forfeit all his estates, but he recovered them when the Duke was executed. The Earl was a good landlord, generous, affectionate and very popular.

Edward, 17th Earl of Oxford, was born in 1550 and succeeded his father in 1562 at the age of twelve. At once he became a Royal Ward under the care of Sir William Cecil, Lord Burghley, the Queen's Treasurer, and went to live in London with George Gascoigne, the poet, at Cecil House in the Strand. It is recorded that "On the 3rd day of September, 1562, came riding out of Essex from the funeral of his father, the young Earl of Oxford, with seven score horse all in black; through London and Chepe to Ludgate, and so to Temple Bar; between five and six of the afternoon."

There is an immense amount known about

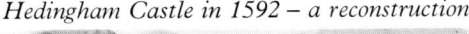

Hedingham Castle in 1592 – a reconstruction

this brilliant and accomplished man and yet there are some strange and unexplained silences in his life. By many he is identified as the true author of the Shakespeare plays. Conclusive proof is lacking, but there is a great deal of circumstantial evidence. In June, 1586, Queen Elizabeth granted him £1,000 a year until he died, and she expressly stated that the Earl was not to be called upon by the Exchequer to render any account as to its expenditure. It has been suggested that this money was granted to Oxford to enable him to provide dramatic entertainment at Court.

He spent much time with his uncle, Arthur Golding, a learned and clever man, who acted as his tutor. It is interesting that Golding translated Ovid's *Metamorphoses* from Latin into English, and the author of the Shakespeare plays made great use of this translation. He was an unusually intelligent child and had gained degrees from both Oxford and Cambridge by the age of sixteen. An attractive boy, with brown curly hair and hazel eyes, he became a great favourite of Queen Elizabeth and would go up river to Richmond to dance with her or play the virginals. "My Turk" she called him. In Tournaments, a very popular pastime, he was frequently the victor, and in 1571 the Queen presented him with the chief prize at the Joust in Westminster.

He travelled extensively in France and Italy; both countries were enjoying a time of great artistic development and he felt compelled to study the architecture, the painting and the literature first hand. De Vere played his part in the defence of his country, and in 1585 he commanded an expedition with Robert, Earl of Leicester to help with the relief of the states of Holland from the domination of the Spaniards. Three years later "at his own charge and in pure love of his country" he hired and fitted out a ship, probably the Edward Bonaventure, and joined the grand fleet sent to oppose the Spanish Armada. Oxford enjoyed the game of real tennis and once, playing before the Queen in a match against Sir Philip Sidney, a disagreement occurred and he called Sidney "a puppy". The Queen took the side of de Vere, which so annoyed Sir Philip that he departed in a sulk to

The 17th Earl, possibly the true author of the 'Shakespeare' plays

Wilton, where he occupied his time to good advantage and wrote the poem "Arcadia".

Edward de Vere, nicknamed "The Spendthrift", made some unlucky investments and lost considerable sums of money in backing the voyages of Frobisher, which proved to be total financial disasters. He liked to live in magnificent style, and his extravagance undoubtedly depleted the family fortunes and led to the sale of numerous estates. There is an interesting account of a journey to London, when de Vere was seen "Riding into the city and to his house by London Stone, with four score gentlemen in front of him in livery of Reading tawny with chains of gold about their necks, and behind him one hundred tall yeomen all in the like livery, without chains, but all having his cognizance of the Blue Boar embroidered on their left shoulder."

He married Anne Cecil, daughter of his guardian, Lord Burghley, and they had three daughters. She died in 1588, and he then married Elizabeth Trentham, one of the Queen's Maids of Honour, and they had a son, Henry, who became the 18th Earl after his father's death in 1604. From about 1591 Oxford's life becomes a mystery, and little is known about him for his last thirteen years.

Henry, 18th Earl of Oxford, was the last de Vere to own and live at Hedingham Castle. In his youth he was said to have had debauched and riotous ways, but when his mother died and he inherited a share of her fortune he went abroad for five years. When he returned in 1618 he was

The 18th Earl of Oxford, the last Earl to own the Castle

reported to have changed so much that he was "refined in every esteem". In 1622 he was Vice-Admiral of a Fleet patrolling the Channel, but he indiscreetly criticised the Buckingham predominance when intoxicated, and was imprisoned in the Tower for nearly two years. Soon after his release, on 1st January, 1624, he married Diana Cecil, daughter of the Earl of Exeter, an heiress and a great beauty of the time. He died of a fever the following year, after wounds received at the Battle of the Hague. His body was brought home to England and buried in St. John the Baptist's Chapel in Westminster Abbey, on July 15th, 1625. When Lord Oxford died of wounds, the Hedingham Castle estate

passed to Elizabeth Trentham and away from the de Vere family. It was in 1616, during the 18th Earl's lifetime, that the church tower at Hedingham was rebuilt onto the Norman nave, almost certainly with bricks from the towers near the Keep. The West window is reputed to have originally been in the large Tudor Hall at the Castle, and the various badges of the de Veres can be seen above it.

Robert, 19th Earl of Oxford, who succeeded his 2nd cousin, was born at Hedingham in about 1575. It is recorded that when the news came to him of his cousin Henry's death he exclaimed "that he was then the poorest Earl in England." He took his seat in the House of Lords in 1626 and was knighted on 3rd May, 1629. From then until his death three

St. Stephen's Chapel, Bures, where the surviving de Vere monuments are gathered

years later he was Lt.-Col of an English regiment in Holland under his cousin, Lord Vere of Tilbury. He was shot through the head and was probably buried on the battlefield.

His heir, Aubrey, was born in London in 1627.

Aubrey, 20th Earl of Oxford, was in 1660 appointed Lord Lieutenant of Essex. He was made Colonel of the Royal Regiment of Horse (from then on Oxford's Horse or Oxford's Blues, now the Horse Guards) on its formation, 26th January, 1661. At the coronations of James II and William and Mary he bore the Sword of State. James needed an obedient Parliament and tried to use the Lord Lieutenants of the counties to ensure the return of picked men. When asked of his intentions by the King, Oxford's answer was, "Sir, I will stand by your Majesty against all enemies to the last drop of my blood, but this is a matter of conscience, and I cannot comply." This displeased the King, and de Vere's regiment was taken from him and Lord Petre replaced him as Lord Lieutenant. Oxford went over to Prince William of Orange, who when he became King William III reinstated him in all his previous positions and made him Lt.-General of Horse and Foot. He fought at the Battle of the Boyne in 1690, and was Speaker of the House of Lords from 1st August 1700 to 18th September, 1701. He died at his house in Downing Street, on 12th March, 1703, aged seventy-six, and was buried in Westminster Abbey in the same vault as his kinsman, Sir Francis Vere. On his death, the Earldom of Oxford, created in 1142, became extinct, though the representation of the family passed through his daughter, Lady Diana de Vere, to the Dukes of St. Albans.

The 20th and last Earl of Oxford

Hedingham Church whose tower was rebuilt by the 18th Earl

Sir Robert Ashhurst and some of his friends in front of his new house in 1719

After the death of the 18th Earl's widow, the Castle reverted by family arrangement to the widow of the 17th Earl – Elizabeth Trentham, who in 1713 sold the estate for the first time in 550 years. The purchaser was Sir William Ashhurst, M.P. and Lord Mayor of London in 1693. He married Elizabeth Thompson and had seven sons and six daughters. As soon as he bought Hedingham he proceeded to build himself a new, more convenient modern house near to the great Keep on the Outer Bailey. This was in the reign of Queen Anne and the house is a fine example of the architecture of that date. Sir William died in 1719, the year the building was completed, and there is a drawing of his eldest son, Sir Robert, showing off his new house to friends. Robert died in 1726 and was succeeded by his brother William. Sadly, the seven brothers were not long-lived as Hedingham was inherited by Sir William's only daughter Elizabeth, who married Sir Henry Hoghton, Bt., of Hoghton Tower. They in turn had an only daughter Elizabeth, who married Mr. Lewis Majendie.

The Majendie family lived at Hedingham for several generations and in 1870 Lewis Ashhurst Majendie married Lady Margaret Lindsay, daughter of the 25th Earl of Crawford and Balcarres. Miss Musette Majendie, a descendant, left Hedingham Castle to the Hon. Thomas Lindsay, brother of the 29th Earl of Crawford and Balcarres. He is married to Virginia Capel Cure and they have five children, three sons and two daughters.

Mr. Lindsay is descended from the de Veres through both his father's and his mother's families. His father, the 28th Earl of Crawford and Balcarres, was descended from John, 7th Earl of Oxford (1350). His mother, Mary Cavendish, is daughter of Lord Richard Cavendish and his wife Lady Moyra de Vere Beauclerk, daughter of the 10th Duke of St. Albans. Charles Beauclerk, 1st Duke of St. Albans, was the illegitimate son of King Charles II and his mistress Nell Gwynne. On April 3rd, 1694, he married Lady Diana de Vere, eldest daughter and heiress of Aubrey de Vere, 20th and last Earl of Oxford, the final member of one of England's most illustrious noble families. The Duke and Duchess had two sons, and their posterity increased through the ages with the name Beauclerk invariably prefixed by de Vere.